vox poetica
inspirations: images & words
collection 2, fall 2010

ISBN 978-1-936373-05-5

© 2010 Unbound Content, LLC. All rights retained by the original authors and artists with the exception of first-time anthology rights to distribute in this collection. These first-time anthology rights are held by Unbound Content, LLC, published as part of the vox poetica *inspirations* collections.

All images reprinted here are owned by Ian Burden, Bridget Fahey O'Brien, and Bobbie Troy. Permission for use requests will be forwarded.

vox poetica *inspirations: images & words*
collection 2, fall 2010

With much appreciation to **Manny Beltran** for art design consultation, **Ian Burden**, **Bridget Fahey O'Brien** and **Bobbie Troy** for the photographs that inspired these words, and the **writers** and **readers** who share their talents and passions, who give and take, who are the living expression of artistic community.

--Annmarie Lockhart, editor

table of contents

Spring in Madison Square Park

Imitation, by Bob Christin 7
Immortality, by Clarissa McFairy 8
Cherry Blossom Haiku, by Bobbie Troy 8
Cinquain for Spring, by Grace Burns 8
Our Worlds, by Christine Tapson 9
Blossoms Bring New Love, by Jeanette Cheezum 10
Spring's Fleeting Affair, by Mark Gooch 11
Poem for Spring, by Nick Hawkins 12
I Love, New York, by Ray Sharp 13
Over the Rainbow, by Annmarie Lockhart 14
A Spring Seduction, by Phyllis Johnson 15

Sun Vision

A Thousand Suns, by Bobbie Troy 17
Autumn Morning, by Homero Rey 17
Early Morning Light, by Bette Hileman 18
Hester's Surprise, by Annmarie Lockhart 18
La luz del amor se florece, by Ray Sharp 19
Light of the Sun, by Gianluca D'Elia 20
First Visit to Medjugorje, by Grace Burns 21
Cocktail Party, by Clarissa McFairy 22
Life Storeys, by Maxwell van der Gaast 23
I Stand With Giants, by Nick Hawkins 24
Forest of Love, by Mark Gooch 25
The Garden's Keeper, by Orlando Rey 26
A Spring, by John Lavan 27
Letting Go, by Jack Daily...27
Sunrise, by Jeanette Cheezum 27
They Said It Was Coming, by Cassie Premo Steele 28

Frames Sunset

Taps, by Jeanette Gallagher... 31
Missing Sunlight, by Marla Deschenes... 32
And There I Lay, by Nick Hawkins 33
We Are Alone, by Neil Ellman 33
Direction Is Everything, by Jack Daily 34
Orange and black, by Kay Middleton 34
Entrapment, by Bobbie Troy 35
Our Walk Together, by Ray Sharp 35
Revision 10.2, by Grace Burns 35
Flights, by Holly Schullo 36
Structure of Life, by Mark Gooch 37
Mysteries Behind Doors, by Rae Spencer 38
Riker's Island, Open Air, by Annmarie Lockhart 38
At Rest, by Cassie Premo Steele 39
Love Thy Children, by Jeanette Cheezum 40
Emotional Terrorism, by Lisa Nielsen 40
Quitting Time, by Joanna S Lee 41
American Pride, by Mildred Speidel...41
Only the Stars Shall Weep, by Clarissa McFairy 42
Being Brave, or Not, by Christine Tapson...43
A Place Where the Devil Reigns, by James G Piatt....................................44

Spring in Madison Square Park

Photo by Bridget Fahey O'Brien

Imitation

By Bob Christin

If purple is passion,
this is an erotic display
of the last act of intercourse,
following foreplay and
entanglement,
these purple leaves
portray the explosion,
the climax of pleasure
and reveal to us
that nature imitates
life's joys in pleasure
as tsunamis imitate
emotional storm clouds
of anger and violence.

Immortality
By Clarissa McFairy

cherry blossom love
beside me
bright sky above
so fancy free
you, me, and Immortality

now it's just you and me
walking in the park
where Spring has sprung
but Youth has passed
it could not last

under this tree
cherry blossoms fell
from your tumbling hair
as I twirled you
in the air

that bench where we sat
is still there
kissed by the sun
and warmed by laughter
forever after

for love leaves
a stirring in the trees
an energy in the air
and cherry blossoms
forever in your hair

Cherry Blossom Haiku
By Bobbie Troy

cherry blossoms hide
like children in a crowd
waiting to burst forth

Cinquain for Spring
By Grace Burns

Blue sky
sparkling, purples
popping, sun kissing bare
skin. Omnipresent signs of life
anew.

vox poetica

Our Worlds
By Christine Tapson

What on earth happened
to the Earth?
What were we doing
while SHE was preparing
for an explosion?

Because we carry briefcases
catch taxis
talk-arrange-debate
shop-cook-clean
we didn't even notice.

And all the while,
in our busy-blindness,
our Earth Mother
was preparing
to Gift us.

How did we MISS the blossoms?
About what were we thinking?

Why did we only see them
when they exploded
in our face?

What were we doing
that was so important
while Mother Earth
prepared to give birth?

HER Gift is Awareness
of what is important.
All we're concerned with
is ourselves,
our own mortality.

And while we read
with dispassion
about the death
of strangers,
our own Mother could die.

Blossoms Bring New Love

By Jeanette Cheezum

Winter had died and
so had her husband.
She came to his favorite
park where blossoms
bloomed with new hope.

Squirrels scampered to
collect her offerings … she
felt it her duty to carry on
her beloved's traditions.

Sunlight dimming and an
empty bag, she grabbed her
walker. Before she could
move the friendliest squirrel
stopped her—just as a branch
dropped behind him.

Was it Bill?

Spring's Fleeting Affair
By Mark Gooch

Palette of colors,
vibrant and rich
spring is the painter
whose purpose is clear:
remove Old Man Winter
his sleigh and reindeer

Mother Nature has arrived
displaying her charms
voyeurs ogle the view
reach out for a feel

beautiful fabric unfurls from bud
endowed with sensuous pleasures
designed to entice and embrace
the bees while they dance

softly whisper
to all as they pass
don't hurry my friend
we aren't here for long
revel in my beauty
drink my intoxicating bouquet
for soon I will be gone
with only memories
for us to share

vox poetica

Poem for Spring

By Nick Hawkins

I embrace my eyes to see
Maiden of beauty I so do feel
Sitting on my brow you deliver spring.

Amongst polluted diversions of reality
I can touch lilac silk with porcelain fingers
Winter has slipped silently behind your curtain.

Smiles are borne through image of sun drenched memories
Breathing on days we promise to love forever
Living is for the blind who see only what nature senses.

I open my eyes to darkness
I'm awake again, kept from spring by lack of sight
And the maiden of beauty I do so feel.

I Love, New York
By Ray Sharp

New York breathes through her trees
like this cherry in full blossom

    (or is it crab apple?
    Your sneezes are indiscriminate
    and blooming like _____ trees.)

Some kind of shaggy dog
is watering the tulips (irises?)
Of this much I am certain:

    we are sharing the best hot pretzel ever,
    and watching you lick mustard
    from the corner of your mouth--
    there, you did it again--
    makes my breath come in gusts
    like the spring wind,
    makes my heart flower purple and pink

in the middle of this brick and steel city.

Over the Rainbow
By Annmarie Lockhart

It's as if the world has
gone from gray to color
like in The Wizard of Oz.
Birds and people have
come to life and we are
all over the rainbow.

A world gone mad
verdant with color.

Cherry trees strip tease
and litter the lawn with
petals pink and white.
They fall beside me
whispering the forgotten
news that Barry is dead.

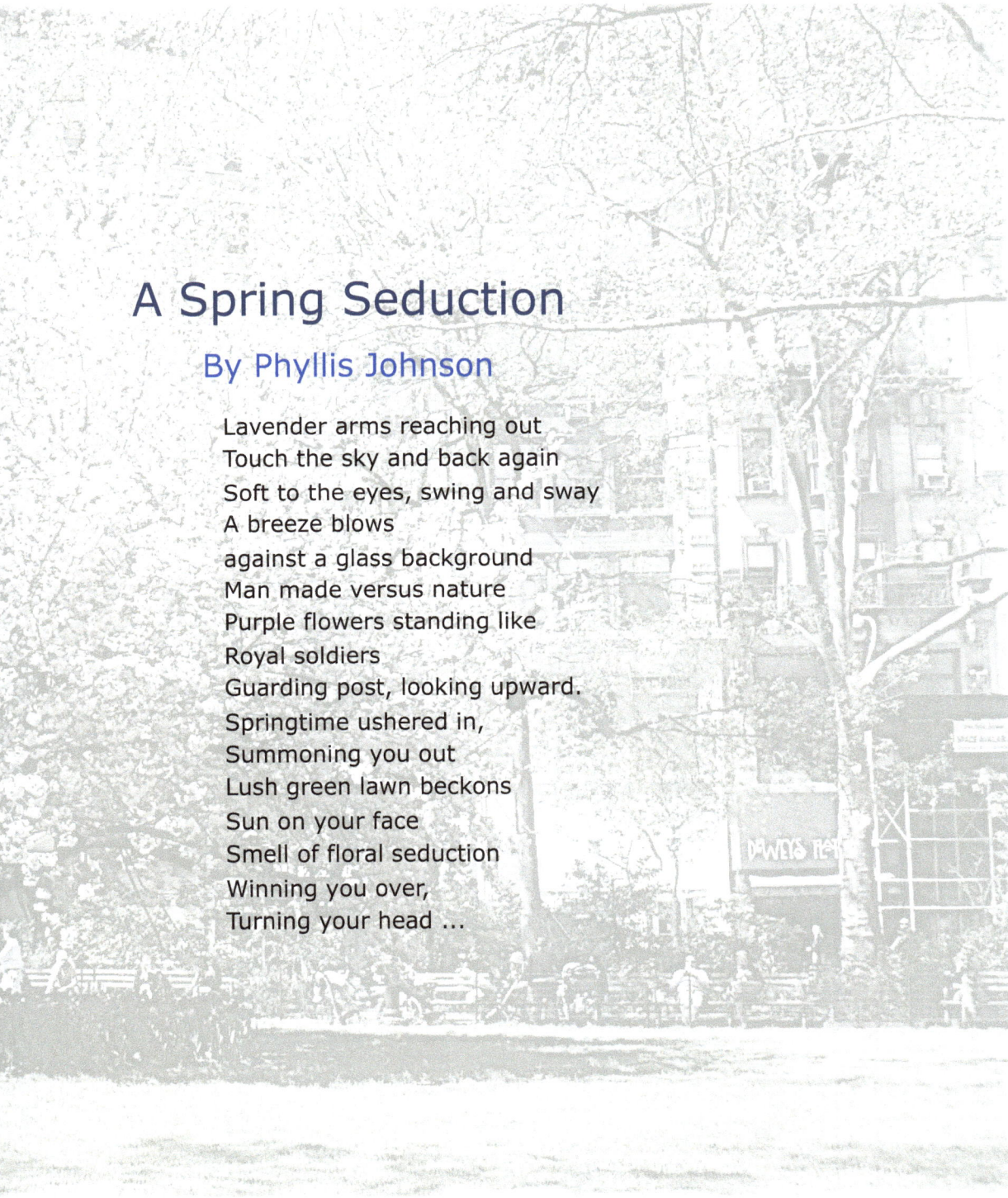

A Spring Seduction
By Phyllis Johnson

Lavender arms reaching out
Touch the sky and back again
Soft to the eyes, swing and sway
A breeze blows
against a glass background
Man made versus nature
Purple flowers standing like
Royal soldiers
Guarding post, looking upward.
Springtime ushered in,
Summoning you out
Lush green lawn beckons
Sun on your face
Smell of floral seduction
Winning you over,
Turning your head …

Sun Vision

Photo by Bobbie Troy

A Thousand Suns

By Bobbie Troy

a thousand suns
pass my morning window
memories of you

Autumn Morning

By Homero Ray

crisp autumn morning
sunlight streaming through the trees
I am filled with hope

vox poetica

Early Morning Light
By Bette Hileman

What fascinates me is early morning light
in the forest outside the living room window.
Every time I see it, it seems magical.

One morning I saw three deer in that light,
looking at me through the trees.
I walked out on the front porch.
They stayed there,
Standing still, staring at me,
as if I did not belong.

Hester's Surprise
By Annmarie Lockhart

when the sun
breaks white
through
the shade
of centuries-old
trees
she sees
his heart
as if it
weren't
bound in
black cloth
and dry leather
but beating
in this moment
strong and free

inspirations: images & words

vox poetica

La luz del amor se florece
(The Light of Love Is Blooming)
By Ray Sharp

El sol se florece por los árboles
en forma de la verdadera cruz,
como el amor se crece
en la jaula vacia de mis costillos
y se convierte en corazón vivo—
¡un milagro!—con cuatro cámaras
de sangre y un centro de luz brillante.

El alquimia del amor se transforma
los huesos a madera,
la madera a la cruz,
el crucificado a dios,
y Dios a la luz que es amor,
un círculo eternal que se florece
como el sol por los árboles.

The sun is blooming through the trees
in the shape of the True Cross,
like the love that grows
in the empty cage of my ribs
and becomes a living heart—
A miracle!—with four chambers
of blood and a center of brilliant light.

The alchemy of love changes
bones into wood,
wood into a cross,
the crucified into a god,
and God into the light that is love,
an endless circle that blooms
like sunlight through the trees.

inspirations: **images & words**

Light of the Sun
By Gianluca D'Elia

The worst thing everyday is
When the sun shines its light
It blinds my eyes
As I wake up and sigh
It pours through the window
At the break of dawn

The worst thing everyday is
When the sun shines its light
Go away
Leave me alone
For you have ruined the darkness
Why must you give mercy?
Can't you see I'd rather bare my own sins?
I am not afraid of all the casting shadows
At the end of colorful rainbows
There are dark skies

I don't need protection
I am not safe as it is
I don't want to let in the light
I only dream of the night

Because the light blinds my eyes
It seduces and lies
With promises of good
Where is the night that I used to know?
At last, I will shut my eyes.

First Visit to Medjugorje
By Grace Burns

I stand
on the side
of the mountain
searching for a sign.
Those around me see
divine visions
that I cannot see.
They hear
messages of peace
that I cannot hear.
I do not belong here.
I am unworthy.
I am unloved.
I am alone.

vox poetica

Cocktail Party*
By Clarissa McFairy

a forest of faces
telling tall stories
pleasantries
small talk
call it what you will

this is how we stand
at cocktail parties
rooted to the spot
our true colours
hidden

by superimpositions
painted smiles
and cubic zirconias
in place of eyes
that flit and flutter

around the room
looking for birds
of a feather
who usually flock
together

but every now and then
among the familiars
an alien lands
and two people
across a room

have a flash
of recognition
it only takes a moment
to recognise a stranger
you have known forever

Life Storeys*
By Maxwell van der Gaast

Pine trees;
apartment blocks
in wood

housing many forms
of Life
at various levels

from lower ground
to sunroof
little worms

and wood-boring beetles
flying insects
and the dreaded spider

squirrels gathering nuts
from their private pantry
of pine cones

lyric song birds
of many hues
and the peasant pigeon

and at nightfall
the owl sits gazing
at the grass floor below

yet midst this life
and death
is a natural harmony

not found in blocks
of concrete and steel
where man covets

and plots and plans
fearful of the morrow
in clothes of sorrow

*The writers are using Standard South African English.

vox poetica

I Stand With Giants
By Nick Hawkins

I stand with giants,
Mother Nature's sentinels,
They covet thy soul and gather moss amongst themselves

Blazes of streaming trails,
And the sentinels afford protection.
For their own remain diligent in refrain.

She stands with giants,
Adorned in garlands of her own dawn,
Quiet in her delicate beauty.

Absorbing vast attributes of the largest star
She caresses light into being
And her sentinels breathe life.

I am giant,
She takes my hand and leads me to her sanctuary.
Inhaling her scents, I exhale with contentment to protect her.

Standing tall, omnipresence infuses smiles
The sentinels call to arms
I stand with giants.

Forest of Love
By Mark Gooch

Trees move aside
When the Sun takes control
Brilliant and white
Providing life to the creatures below.

We lie here together
Looking up to the sky
Holding on to each other
Wishing this day never dies.

Here war isn't allowed.
Or hate and distrust
Just two who are lovers
With a little time we can share.

Welcome to our slice of heaven
Our haven of LOVE
Protected by trees
And watched over by the Sun.

vox poetica

The Garden's Keeper
By Orlando Rey

Forms of light are my children
total dependency
from cradle to grave
oblivious to their fate.

Take what it takes
my commands are kept
not even the nights flow
without my consent.

From where I come from
I was told to share
what I was given
not a God!

No one master my garden
Uniqueness of creation
I tend it like I should
nothing will survive my absence.

I respond to the name:
AMON RA...
All mighty SUN

vox poetica

A Spring
By John Lavan

evening stills;
trees—wetted with rain—
stand and face a purple sun.

Listen to calls
pulse—a swell of birds
flickering nuances
cooing, echoing
beating little hearts

(inside my skull
I also am wittering and twittering)

Overhead; leaves lurch
wave on turning ocean wave
beckoning ight: moving church,
urging Nature, lusting life.

Letting Go
By Jack Daily

Wet underbrush
Clinging
Holding on
Step into the light
Let go

Brighter days
Are best
I see the sun
Can you?

Feel the warmth
As trees surround
Just find a path
Dark fades too

Sunrise
By Jeanette Cheezum

I could hear the wolf howling through the tall pines trying to hide from the sun so as not to wither away.

I laugh at him now, he couldn't tantalize. His fangs always taunting but I am wise. Never trust him or his lies …

I'll look to the sun to protect me while I walk through the pines.

inspirations: images & words

They Said It Was Coming

By Cassie Premo Steele

They said it would start with light
and
geometry.
They said we would
see the beauty
of math.
The pattern
underneath everything.
The circles
and lines
connecting living things.
The random
would have order.
Objects would speak.
Doubters
would break down.
Years
of fears lifted,
every end seen
as something
new.
They said it was coming.
It's here now
Can you see it?
Can you?

Frames Sunset

Photo by Ian Burden

Taps
By Jeanette Gallagher

Yellow clouds gather in a gray sky,
Reflecting the beauty of twilight.
Diffused light obscures the source
For grief and lack of solace.

An uncertain breeze brings cause
For a stalwart flag to bend and sway,
And nearby a mother chokes back sobs

While her son's ashes float across the sea,
And one lone gull flies above to declare
Dignity over injustice of war.

Then heard near the shore
The bugle's sound of Taps,
Day is done, gone the sun.

Missing Sunlight
By Marla Deschenes

There is quiet here
Only the softest whispered disturbance of the salty breeze,
Ruffling the ratty remnants
Of someone's once beloved remembrance.

I will hold your hand
Brush dirt from in between fingers, hold abandoned thoughts
No sounds but the gulls and our hearts beating
Secluded from the world only here.

Lay me down
Quiet in the shadowy cast of the pier.
Trace my body with seashells and fingertips and breath.
The diminishing light calls us home.

vox poetica

And There I Lay
By Nick Hawkins

And there I lay …
Life remains still
Thoughts breathe, light winds eclipse moments
Sun warms a brow, melting days
Eyes close soft.

Silence is louder than noise
Inner visions wash shores
And there I lay …

Solitude is one within this ambered eve
I fall graciously into nowhere
Where is love, where was war
Yet lying beneath earth's cradle I cry …

Grieving isn't giving up, just as living isn't life
And there I lay …

We Are Alone
By Neil Ellman

So it has come to this—
The city gone
In an instant
Like Pompeii
buried under the ash
Of its own excess.
Where children begged
For pennies
And women, like me,
For bread
We would trade
Our souls
And we often did.
We would abide
By the law
Of supply and demand.
The elders said
Follow our book
And we tried
And now
Their flag hangs limply
In the windless sky
And the sun sets
For one last time.

inspirations: images & words

Direction Is Everything
By Jack Daily

If my head faces East
I see hope, beginnings
I get my tools and thump my chest

If my head faces West
I see an unfinished day in ruins
I go fetal and close my eyes

If my head faces North
I see promise on the left
I must weigh action
      against consequence

If my head faces South
I feel awash in warm salt water
And this day will last forever

Orange and black
By Kay Middleton

The wire taut—or taught
communication strained
thin & tight against the fire
edges night's knife.

Our bars not
always definable
stark instead
at times of change
those dawns and dusks
when the light
is sharp before
desertion.

Our prisons not
always visible
incarceration of
circumstance occasional
enough to be
disregarded and escape
postponed.

Entrapment
By Bobbie Troy

i warned you:
capturing my heart
would be like
trying to trap
the setting sun

i warned you
but you didn't listen

Our Walk Together
By Ray Sharp

You know our reality is built up stilt by stick,
a scaffold that frames the space of our existence
between sea and sky, sun rays and tattered flags.
This life we lead is an intrepid pier above dark water,
a long walk under the banking wind-held gulls.

Revision 10.2
By Grace Burns

My concept was brilliant.
My specifications were perfectly articulated
and strictly adhered to.
The raw materials used were of the highest quality.

Yet my creation did not turn out the way I had envisioned.
Here I sit—
revisiting and revising my drawings and schematics—
searching for Eureka.

Flights
By Holly Schullo

Here is the violin of nature, wooden map
of colors we learned to trust in accordion

songs, cadence of bayou, how you came
and went, and I watched starbirds sculpt

on highways and ladders, wheat dancers
turned earth to corn, until I could not see

anymore. I heard hours open and close
their suitcases and doors in upright bass

and trumpet, touched stairs that led
to gates and porches and bridges until

voices rung from empty tables, weighted
mirrors and shadows, catfish and oranges,

until gull moon played cards with Jesus ...

Structure of Life
By Mark Gooch

The sun continues its vigil
Watching from afar,
Like a medieval sentry
As it makes its daily rounds

No concern about the purpose
About the future or the past
Providing light that creates shadows
On time-worn wooden beams

Listen close,
Its sobs you'll hear
Solitude and silence
Is the greatest fear
Days of waste
Turn to years

This shell does have a purpose
A lesson for all to learn

vox poetica

Mysteries Behind Doors
By Rae Spencer

I always knew
that behind some unseen door
Waited all the long days of my happiness

So I searched
For my shadowed sill of dreams

I opened the squeaking screen
Of my childhood home
And raced boldly free

I dared my knuckles at love's iron gate
And allowed myself to pause
In infatuation's den

Unnumbered, lovely failures
Bright joys I could not hold
Restless hungers I could not sate

Rough frame of contemplation
For a room that needs no doors

I'm inviting you in
To visit
Or stay

To share
All the long days of my happiness

Riker's Island, Open Air
By Annmarie Lockhart

The walls are porous
and the light shines in
circulating sea breeze
and blue sky,

and there are no chains
nor shackles here, no
visible cuffs that bind
and hold.

But this frame contains
my every dream and pins
my skyward wings. It is
a prison,

a breach-proof hold, a keep
hemming me in, locking me
deep inside my unbarred
jail cell.

At Rest
Cassie Premo Steele

No rest is worth anything
    except the rest that is earned.
      —Jean Paul Sartre

Oh, I earned it. I learned it early,
this building and buttressing and holding
what other mothers might have kept
folded over and blanketed for safe
keeping. I was raised to greet the sun
on the run like a prisoner escaping
from everything he'd ever done.
I never stopped to ask my crime.
I took it for granted that I'd do my time.

And now the time has come. I am resting.
Oh, I earned it. I learned it early, this "Say,
can you see" song, the battle went on and
on, and now I am done. Too many deaths.
Too much has died. It isn't a matter of
trying. I tried. We tried. It's time for it
to be over. Another dawn will not
give birth to another battle. It is time to rest.
Imagine it. This is what peace is worth.

vox poetica

Love Thy Children
By Jeanette Cheezum

Mother held her babies to her breast
and tried to guide them to do their best.

Father taught sports and responsibility
to make them strong.

Leaders decided to send them to war.
So money flowed and blood was shed.

Opposing forces left their children mangled
and dead, parents no longer held them to their chest.

Leaders should sit in shame, our countries
never tame—only pass on the blame.

emotional terrorism
By Lisa Nielsen

those once terrorized find their safe place
in the brutal underpinnings of chaos
the familiar
the solace of having been there before

but on spindly legs my heart crawls from the wreckage
only to find that safe haven is an urban myth
like the blanketed yearnings of the sun to comfort you
while leaving you burned

Quitting Time
By Joanna S Lee

A tired whistle blast signals work
day's end; craneman pulls back tight,
parting the cloudbank and revealing a
miracle of molecules: the liquid heat
of a fragmented spectrum pouring
its reds and yellows down
into a ravished earth
of worms and rust;

just another dying sun
bounded by girders of steel
and the sweat of man's delusions.

American Pride
By Mildred Speidel

I walked along the path
Where once he walked that day
I gazed into the sun drenched sky
The flag was now displayed
I held the hand of my child so dear
And kissed his face so sweet
Reminding him that someone died
To make freedom here complete
The rubble a reminder
Of what occurred that day
But now we look once more with pride
Red, white, and blue displayed.

vox poetica

Only the Stars Shall Weep
By Clarissa McFairy

what flag is this
clinging to a pole?
is it my spirit
unfurling
in the fading light

or is this bright hanky
waving goodbye
to an ebbing dream;
flapping more frantically
as it becomes a speck

on the horizon
of sunken dreams?
maybe it's a pole dancer
dancing to a tune
I cannot hear

as I sit here
on this skeleton
of a memory
that once had bones
and blood

and a heartbeat,
a feeble flutter now
as night's cloak covers
our lambent-lidded love
in glistening tears

Being Brave, or Not
By Christine Tapson

We sit behind these bars and fences
And we look.

We're restricted, contained, refrained
Constrained
But we can see.

We can dream
We can remember
We can plan
And look forward.

But we sit behind these bars and fences
And we look.

Sleep tight.
Wherever it is you might seek a dream
I'll meet you there.

vox poetica

A Place Where the Devil Reigns
By James G Piatt

As the golden orb heaves its final sigh
And dips slowly into the darkness of the abyss
Near the East River and Queens where jets
Spew their acrid ashes a dark edifice
Of lost souls slowly fades into a
Soul wrenching aching darkness

A gloomy obscurity paces the dreary halls
Of misery from the infirmed north to
The unhealthy and contagious west
A lonely flag beams silently in the glow
As if incarceration was an answer to
Man's infamous and evil behavior

A Rebel ghost roams the desolate halls
Of Tayler sentenced youth to the
Singer House of sad and fallen ladies
Inside gray buildings past memories of
Raging angry youth plied by Nicholson
Playing his sadistic Program's game reside

How can a civilized society ever
Believe that such inhumane systems
Solve the problems of dysfunctional families
Poverty abuse and mental illness
When will we who profess freedom
Solve our crime problems without revenge

When will America cease to be the world leader
In executions and incarcerations of those
In a society who need to be saved and healed
Not killed and placed in Hell's cells where
There is no opportunity for rehabilitation
When will we stop the barbarous insanity

The Contributors

Ian Burden lives in Finland and works as a freelance media professional on voiceovers, short films, and photography for corporate clients. He believes in the spoken word and his poetry CD will be available in 2011.

Grace Burns is an automation and validation engineer, technical writer, mobile DJ, creative writer, and mother of two. She lives and works in New Jersey.

Jeanette Cheezum is a writer of all types of fiction and poetry. Her work has been published at several online journals and in 2 *vox poetica* anthologies. She is a member of Hampton Roads Writers (see a list of her published work at their site, www.hamptonroadswriters.org.)

Robert Christin is a retired English professor (Ohio State University, Notre Dame, Pace University, New York University). He has taught creative writing at the Adult Learning Center in Virginia Beach for more than 10 years. He is the founder and lead mentor of The Albright Poets. His work has been widely published and he is writing a book-length literary memoir.

Jack Daily is a writer and photographer. Born in Birmingham AL, he has lived and worked in Miami and Washington DC in the medical and space industries. He is a member of the Alexandria Art League and the Windmore Foundation of the Arts. His photos have been included in art shows and his writing was published in *Images in Ink* (Windmore Foundation of the Arts, Culpeper VA, 2010).

Gianluca D'Elia is a freelance writer, high school student, and Euro-pop know-it-all. In the future he hopes to publish a book and become a political activist and interior designer. He resides in a suburb outside of New York with his family and an energetic young Italian Greyhound. His work has appeared at *Caper Literary Journal* and *vox poetica*.

Marla Deschenes writes from her punk rock hideout located in suburban Enfield CT. Her work has been published at *vox poetica* and *SPARK*. She is working on a personal zine (Bandages of Words) and 30 Poems in 30 Days.

Neil Ellman is a retired educator living and writing in New Jersey. He has published numerous poems and his 4 chapbooks are collections of poems based on works of modern art. His most recent chapbook is *The Great Metaphysician and Other Ekphrastic Inventions* (Erbacce Press, 2010).

Jeanette Gallagher moved to Virginia Beach at 10 and grew up in a family-run, ocean-front hotel. She is a retired therapist who worked at Tidewater Psychiatric Institution and Center of Behavioral Medicine. She is a member of the Albright Poets and Hampton Roads Writers.

Mark Gooch is business manager of a medium-sized corporation in Lansing MI. He lives in Clio MI with his wife Pam and is a graduate of the Bentley School System in Burton MI. His poetry journey began with the mentoring of 2 friends.

Nick Hawkins believes poetry is born rather than created. He writes responsive and rhyming poetry and experiments with other forms. He is from Brighton, England and he and his wife Anita have 3 children and 2 grandchildren.

Bette Hileman is a writer and photographer who divides her time between Reston and Culpeper County VA. For 27 years she wrote for *Chemical & Engineering News*. She is working on her second novel. Her photos have been exhibited at Ice House Gallery in Washington VA and Windmore Foundation for the Arts in Culpeper. She co-edited *Images in Ink*, an anthology by the Pen-to-Paper writing group (Windmore Foundation, 2010).

Phyllis Johnson is a poet, author, and photojournalist living in Virginia. Creativity rocks her world. Her published works are *Being Frank with Anne*, *Hot and Bothered by It*, and *Twelve Is for More Than Doughnuts*. She is marketing a young adult suspense novel cowritten with award-winning writer Nancy Naigle.

John Lavan is a poet living in the UK, who practices writing at least 1 poem a day. His passion is words and working through them to feeling. His family is his inspiration.

Joanna S Lee has never been formally trained in any kind of writing, thank you very much. She can, however, dissect the brainstem of a neonatal mouse or diagnose your lower back pains. Her first full-length book of poetry, *the somersaults I did as I fell,* (iColor, Richmond VA) was released in 2009. Visit her blog, arspoetica.wordpress.org.

Annmarie Lockhart is the founding editor of *vox poetica* and the founder of unbound CONTENT. She has been reading and writing poetry since she could read and write.

Clarissa McFairy (Clare van der Gaast) is a South African journalist living in Cape Town. Her hobbies are painting and writing short stories and French poetry. Her work has appeared in South African anthologies, at *vox poetica*, and in *inspirations: images & words* (collection 1).

Kay Middleton, having lived prior lives on the edges of Michigan, Hawaii, Virginia, and North Carolina, now seeks to center herself. Writing helps, along with copious amounts of coffee on mornings followed by afternoons of champagne with fellow poets, evenings of merlot with fellow novelists, and sleepless nights with Andorra (her muse). Visit her web site: kaymiddleton.net.

Lisa Nielsen was born and bred in Brooklyn NY. She is navigating her way as a single mom living on Staten Island, which can feel at times like a strange version of *Little House on the Prairie* and at other times completely like home.

Bridget Fahey O'Brien is a city life photographer. Her heart and art are rooted in New York and San Francisco. Her work has appeared at *vox poetica, SPARK*, and in the homes of her family and friends.

James G Piatt is a retired professor with degrees from California State Polytechnic University and Brigham Young University. Two of his relatives were prolific poets in the 1800s. He was the featured poet at *Contemporary American Voices* in October 2010 and his work can be read in places such as *Apollo's Lyre*, *A Handful of Stones*, *The Penwood Review*, *WestWard Quarterly*, *Caper Journal*, *Wilderness House*, and *vox poetica*.

Homero Rey is a scientist and part-time poet living in Campbell CA. He is married and has 2 children who inspire him to see joy in the world every day.

Orlando Rey is an American of Cuban extraction. He is a retired engineer and math teacher whose passion for poetry has been with him since his high school days back in Cuba.

Holly Schullo was awarded the Louisiana Literature Poetry Prize (2007) and a Vermont Studio fellowship (2006). Her work has been published in *Literary Mama*, *Louisiana Review*, *Poems and Plays*, *Tigertail*, and other journals. Her poetry manuscript is entitled *Empty Boat at Moonlight*. She teaches gifted and talented students in Evangeline Parish LA.

Ray Sharp composes poems while running, biking, skiing, and race-walking the forested hills of Michigan's Upper Peninsula, writes them in composition books, and types them with his 2 index fingers. Ray's work can be seen at *SPARK*, *Caper Journal*, *Eclectic Flash*, *vox poetica*, *Referential Magazine*, and *quarrtsiluni*; he blogs at raysharp.wordpress.com.

Mildred Speidel lives in Chesapeake VA and is retired. She has loved poetry for as long as she can remember. She writes what she feels; it works for her.

Rae Spencer is a writer and veterinarian living in Virginia. Her poetry has been published in journals such as *The Foundling Review*, *The Glass Coin*, *Grey Sparrow Journal*, *Sliver of Stone*, and *vox poetica*. She was nominated for a Pushcart Prize in 2009.

Cassie Premo Steele's newest collection of poetry, *This is how honey runs* was published by unbound CONTENT in 2010. A frequent contributor to *vox poetica*, she is a Pushcart Prize nominated poet, author of 7 books, and creativity coach who sees clients in person and long distance from her Co-Creating Studio along a little creek in South Carolina. Read her writing and learn about Co-Creating at her web site, www.cassiepremosteele.com.

Christine Tapson is a remedial therapist and educational psychologist who has turned in retirement to farming indigenous African cattle for stud. She lives in a remote area of the Eastern Cape in South Africa, indulging her dream of living surrounded by nature.

Bobbie Troy is a freelance technical editor/writer by day and a writer of flash fiction, poetry, and original fairly tales by night. Her work has appeared online and in print in journals such as *Concise Delight*, *vox poetica*, ArtSPARK, *Haiku Ramblings Journal of Liberal Arts and Education*, and *Leaf Garden*. Her work was nominated in 2009 for a Pushcart Prize.

Maxwell van der Gaast was born in the university town of Stellenbosch, Western Cape, South Africa, where he obtained his LLB. He lives in Cape Town and works as a legal manager. His hobbies are intuitive massage, chilling at the beach, drinking tea, and reading history, especially of the great aerial battles of WWII. He writes poetry when forced to by his wife.

This collection comprises poems inspired by three photographs taken by Ian Burden, Bridget Fahey O'Brien, and Bobbie Troy and posted at the **prompts** page of **vox poetica** in the spring and summer of 2010. After appearing initially at **vox poetica**, prompts images and poems are only available in these *inspirations* collections.

vox poetica is an online literary salon dedicated to bringing poetry into the everyday. **vox poetica** accepts original submissions for publication at the **today's words** and **words to linger on** pages. Poems appearing at these site pages are archived at the **poemblog**.

Read ... write ... share ... be part of the expression experiment!

http://www.voxpoetica.com